W9-AHF-375

SUMMER SMARTS

Activities in Math, Science, Language Arts, and Social Studies to prepare Students for 2nd Grade

WITHDRAWN

JEANNE CRANE CASTAFERO AND JANET VAN RODEN

KINGFISHER

www.houghtonmifflinbooks.com

4/07 13 +T 8.45

Copyright ©1999 by Great Source Education Group, Inc. All rights reserved.

No part of this work may be reproduced or transmitted in any form or by any
means, electronic or mechanical, including photocopying and recording, or by an
information storage or retrieval system without the prior written permission of Great
Source Education Group, Inc. unless such copying is expressly permitted by federal
copyright law. Address inquiries to Permissions, Great Source Education Group, Inc.,
181 Ballardvale Street, Wilmington, MA, 01887.

Portions of this work were originally published as *Unforgettable First.*
Great Source® is a registered trademark of Houghton Mifflin Company.

Printed in India

ISBN: 978-0-7534-6112-9 (Kingfisher)
ISBN: 0-669-46702-2 (Great Source)

Design: Brown Publishing Network, Inc., Diana Maloney
Design Production: Brown Publishing Network, Inc., Joan Paley

Art: **John Magine:** pages 14, 15, 16, 44, 45, 46, 65, 76, 82, 83, 84. **Jen Paley:** pages
2, 4, 5, 25, 29, 35, 37, 55, 73, 77. **Diane Palmisciano:** pages 30, 31, 32, 34, 47, 51,
52, 53, 57, 58, 59, 81, 85, 86, 87, 88. **Tracey Campbell Pearson:** pages 21, 22, 23,
24, 40, 41, 42, 43, 60, 66, 67, 68, 72. **Laura Rader:** pages 8, 9, 10, 11, 36, 38, 54,
56, 74, 75. **Lauren Scheuer:** pages 17, 18, 19, 20, 26, 27, 28, 39, 48, 49, 50.
Nadine Bernard Westcott: pages 3, 6, 7, 12, 13, 33, 61, 62, 63, 64, 69, 70,
71, 80, 89.

Contents

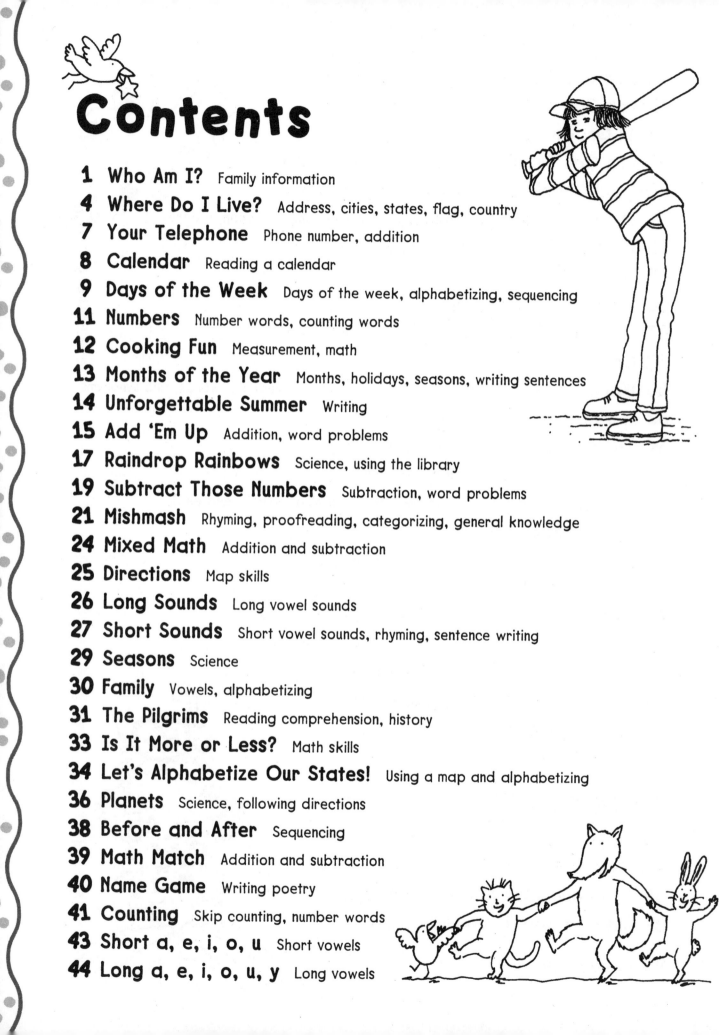

BOOK SECTION

Who Am I?

What is your first name?

_____

What is your middle name?

_____

What is your last name?

_____

How old are you? _____

When is your birthday?

_____

What are the first names of your parents?

_____

_____

What are the first names of your brothers and sisters?

_____

_____

_____

 **Read About It** Read *Do Like Kyla* by Angela Johnson. Is Kyla's family at all like yours?

Draw a picture of yourself.

What three words would you use to describe yourself?

_____, _____, _____

JOKE CORNER

What do you call a sleeping bull? *See page 7 for answer.*

How old is the oldest child in your family? _____

How old is the youngest child in your family? _____

What is the difference in age between the
oldest child and the youngest child? _____

How many brothers live in your house? _____

How many sisters live in your house? _____

How many adults live in your house? _____

How many pets live in your house? _____

What is the total number of people
who live in your house? Don't
forget to count yourself!

_____

3

Where Do I Live?

1. What is your address?

_____
number and street

_____
city or town

_____
state

2. What is the closest big city to your home?

_____

3. Find your state on the map below. Put a red X on it.

4. Find a picture of something that you have done this summer. Paste your summer picture here.

5. In what city or town was this picture taken?

_____

6. In what state was this picture taken?

_____

7. Write a sentence that describes this picture.

_____

_____

_____

The houses, buildings, and land close to your house make up your neighborhood. Several neighborhoods grouped together make up your town or city. Many towns and cities, along with open land, make up states. Fifty states make up our country, the United States of America.

8. What three colors are on our country's flag?

_____

_____

_____

9. You probably have visited a city or town other than your own. Name that city or town and tell what you did there.

_____

_____

10. Name a state that you have visited and tell what you did there.

_____

_____

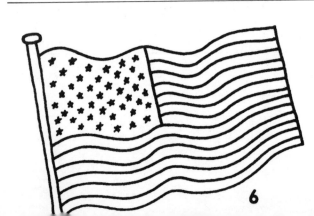

6

Your Telephone

1. What is your phone number?

(___ ___ ___) – ___ ___ ___ – ___ ___ ___ ___

2. How many numbers are in your phone number? _____

3. Add the first two numbers of your phone number.

___ + ___ = ___

4. Add the last two numbers of your phone number.

___ + ___ = ___

5. How many phones do you have in your house? ___

6. In your house, who talks on the phone the most?

_____

Draw a picture of that person talking on the phone.

Answer from page 2: A bulldozer

Calendar

JULY

Sunday	Monday	Tuesday	Wednesday	Thursday	Friday	Saturday
		1	2	3	4	5
6	7	8	9	10	11	12
13	14	15	16	17	18	19
20	21	22	23	24	25	26
27	28	29	30	31		

1. Put a red, a white, and a blue stripe on the 4th of July.

2. Put a yellow star on the first day of July.

3. Color the weekends orange.

4. Put a black X on the last day of July.

5. Write today's date below:

June _____ Wednesday, 2017

(month)   (day)   (year)

Days of the Week

1. Write the days of the week in order, starting with Sunday.

Friday Wednesday Sunday Saturday Tuesday Monday Thursday

Sunday
Monday
Tuesday
Wednesday
Thursday
Friday
Saturday

2. Alphabetize (put in ABC order) the days of the week.

Friday
Monday
Saturday
Sunday
Thursday
Tuesday
Wednesday

3. What two days make up the weekend?

saturday and _Sunday_

4. How many weekdays are there (not including the weekend)? _5_

5. How many days of the week are there? _7_

6. With what three letters do ALL of the days of the week end?

_d_ _a_ _y_

7. Put a number in front of the first, second, third and fourth sentences so the story makes sense.

_4_ Finally, on Saturday, I swam all the way across the pool.

_1_ My swimming lessons began on Monday.

_3_ By Thursday, I knew that I would not drown.

_2_ I wasn't sure by Wednesday that I liked swimming lessons.

Read About It Read *Cookie's Week,* by Cindy Ward, to see what Cookie the cat does on each day of the week.

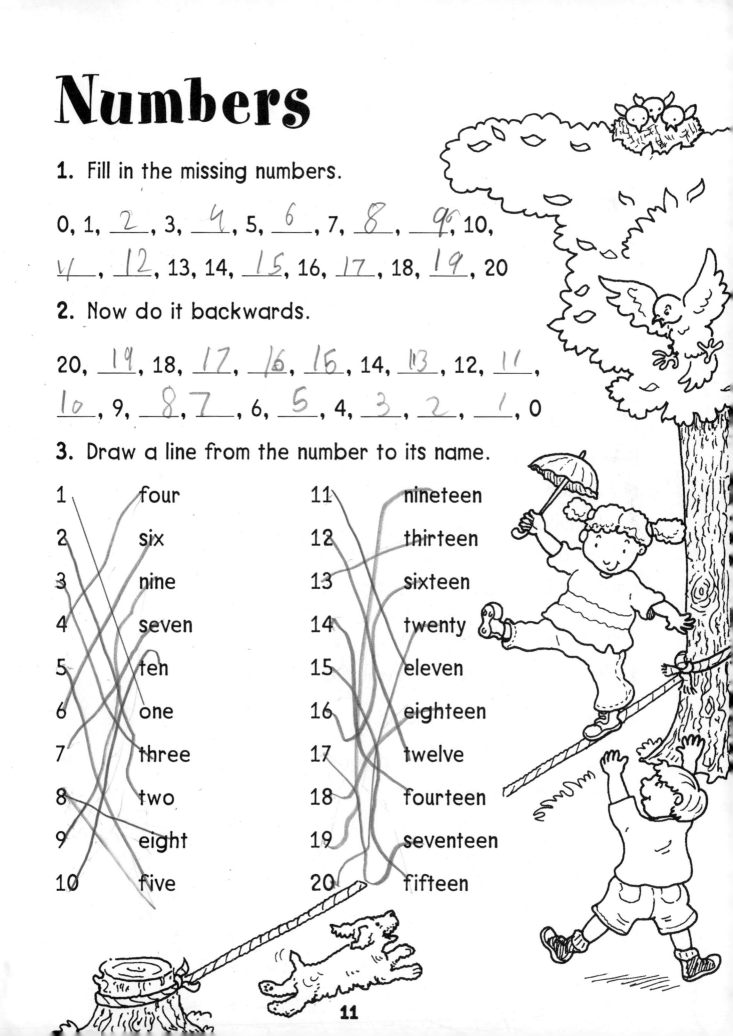

Numbers

1. Fill in the missing numbers.

0, 1, _2_, 3, _4_, 5, _6_, 7, _8_, _9_, 10,
_11_, _12_, 13, 14, _15_, 16, _17_, 18, _19_, 20

2. Now do it backwards.

20, _19_, 18, _17_, _16_, _15_, 14, _13_, 12, _11_,
_10_, 9, _8_, _7_, 6, _5_, 4, _3_, _2_, _1_, 0

3. Draw a line from the number to its name.

1	four	11	nineteen
2	six	12	thirteen
3	nine	13	sixteen
4	seven	14	twenty
5	ten	15	eleven
6	one	16	eighteen
7	three	17	twelve
8	two	18	fourteen
9	eight	19	seventeen
10	five	20	fifteen

Cooking Fun

Here is a recipe for a healthy snack.

YOU WILL NEED
4 tablespoons butter
4 cups Corn Chex cereal
2 cups Wheat Chex cereal
2 cups Rice Chex cereal
3 Tablespoons Sugar
1 teaspoon cinnamon

Have an adult turn on the oven to 325 degrees. Put the butter into a baking pan and melt it in the oven. Add the three kinds of cereals, the sugar, and the cinnamon to the pan and gently mix. Bake for 15 minutes. Now toss the cereal to coat it evenly with the butter. Bake another 15 minutes. Let it cool. Enjoy!

Answer these questions.

1. How many cups of cereal did you use? _____

2. Did you use more sugar or cinnamon? _____

3. How many more tablespoons of butter did
   you use than sugar? _____

Copyright © Great Source

Months of the Year

1. How many months are in the year? _____

2. The months are listed below. Put a number in front of each of them to show the order.

____	February	____	November
____	April	____	December
____	July	____	May
_1_	January	____	October
____	August	____	September
____	March	____	June

3. In what month is your birthday? _____

4. What month is it now? _____

5. How many months is it until your birthday? _____

6. In what month does your school start? _____

7. How many months until school starts? _____

Read About It   Read *Chicken Soup with Rice* by Maurice Sendak and find out how to enjoy chicken soup every month of the year!

Unforgettable Summer

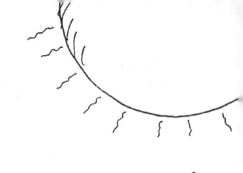

You have just finished first grade. What was the best thing about first grade?

_____

_____

_____

Now it is summer and you have time to play with your friends! Write two sentences about what you like to do with your friends in the summer.

_____

_____

_____

If you could change one thing about your summer, what would it be?

_____

_____

_____

_____

Add 'Em Up

Add.

1.
$$\begin{array}{r} 5 \\ + 3 \\ \hline \end{array} \qquad \begin{array}{r} 8 \\ + 3 \\ \hline \end{array} \qquad \begin{array}{r} 7 \\ + 2 \\ \hline \end{array} \qquad \begin{array}{r} 5 \\ + 5 \\ \hline \end{array} \qquad \begin{array}{r} 2 \\ + 6 \\ \hline \end{array}$$

2.
$$\begin{array}{r} 5 \\ + 7 \\ \hline \end{array} \qquad \begin{array}{r} 8 \\ + 5 \\ \hline \end{array} \qquad \begin{array}{r} 6 \\ + 5 \\ \hline \end{array} \qquad \begin{array}{r} 6 \\ + 7 \\ \hline \end{array} \qquad \begin{array}{r} 9 \\ + 8 \\ \hline \end{array}$$

3.
$$\begin{array}{r} 1 \\ + 9 \\ \hline \end{array} \qquad \begin{array}{r} 8 \\ + 2 \\ \hline \end{array} \qquad \begin{array}{r} 9 \\ + 7 \\ \hline \end{array} \qquad \begin{array}{r} 8 \\ + 8 \\ \hline \end{array} \qquad \begin{array}{r} 6 \\ + 4 \\ \hline \end{array}$$

4. $9 + 6 =$ _____ $6 + 8 =$ _____ $5 + 4 =$ _____

5. $5 + 2 =$ _____ $5 + 9 =$ _____ $3 + 6 =$ _____

6. $3 + 4 =$ _____ $2 + 9 =$ _____ $4 + 8 =$ _____

JOKE CORNER

Why did the burglar take a shower?
See page 19 for the answer.

15

7. Kristin got 1 doll from her parents for her birthday. Then her grandmother gave her 2 more dolls for her birthday. How many dolls did she get for her birthday? _____

8. Elena had 3 baseballs. She found 1 more. Then her friend gave her 2. How many baseballs does she have now?

_____

9. Levar had 4 seashells. He went to the beach and found 10 more. How many seashells does he have now? _____

10. Emily walked 4 blocks from her home to the library. Then she walked 3 more blocks to the movie theater. How many blocks did she walk? _____
If she walks home the same way she came, how many blocks will she walk altogether? _____

Draw your own hot air balloon in the picture above and make it colorful!

Raindrop Rainbows

Sunlight looks white to us. Actually, sunlight is a mixture of different colors—red, orange, yellow, green, blue and violet. This is called the color spectrum. How can we see the beautiful spectrum of colors that make up sunlight? In a rainbow! **A rainbow is a spectrum of sunlight.**

A rainbow is formed when sunlight passes through raindrops. The raindrops bend the light rays and the light rays appear as a spectrum of colors.

Make your own rainbow.

Let's make a rainbow to see how water bends the sunlight into different colors. You will need **sunlight, a small glass bowl with about an inch of water, a mirror, and a piece of white paper.**

Stand your mirror in the water so that it faces the sun. Move your white paper in front of the mirror until you see a rainbow. If you are inside using sunlight through a window, you will not need the white paper. Look for the rainbow on your wall or ceiling.

Rainbows can be seen in many places. Where have you seen a rainbow?

Library Challenge

There are so many wonderful stories and legends about rainbows! Have you ever heard that the rainbow is a bridge to heaven? Or that if you climb up a rainbow it will lead you to a pot of gold?

Go to your library card catalogue or computer search system. Look up the word "rainbow." You will find many selections. Choose a fiction book. What did you find?

Title: _____

Author: _____

What did the story have to do with a rainbow?

_____

_____

_____

_____

Color the six colors of the rainbow above in the order the colors always appear.

18

Subtract Those Numbers

Subtract.

1.
   6   8   6   4   11
− 1   − 5   − 6   − 2   − 3

2.
   8   6   5   12   10
− 4   − 3   − 2   − 8   − 5

3.
   7   9   8   10   9
− 2   − 4   − 3   − 7   − 5

4. $11 - 4 = $ _____ $8 - 6 = $ _____ $12 - 4 = $ _____

5. $9 - 2 = $ _____ $5 - 4 = $ _____ $10 - 8 = $ _____

6. $9 - 8 = $ _____ $12 - 6 = $ _____ $11 - 7 = $ _____

Answer from page 15:
He wanted to make a
clean getaway.

7. Kelly got 7 balloons at the zoo. One balloon flew away. She gave 2 to her friends. How many balloons does she have left? _____

8. James had 10 stickers. He gave 5 to his friend Peter and 1 to his friend Lauren. How many stickers does he have left? _____

9. Peter had 12 baseball cards. He gave 4 to his brother Chris. How many baseball cards does he have now? _____

10. Johnnie had 14 video games. He lost 5 of them. His dog chewed 2 of them. How many games does he have now? _____

20

Mishmash

Circle the two words in each line that rhyme.

1. bone   boy   stone
2. barn   bat   that
3. dish   duck   fish
4. car   star   cat
5. peas   knees   pigs
6. pink   dark   park

These sentences are not correct. Write them correctly.

1. We was going to the beach. _____

_____

2. My mother have red hair. _____

_____

3. This fall, I were be in second grade. _____

_____

Write what these things have in common:

1. spoon   fork   cup   <u>These things are used to eat.</u>

2. apple   orange   pear   _____

3. yellow   green   red   _____

4. February   June   May   _____

5. pants   socks   coat   _____

6. Tuesday   Monday   Friday   _____

7. cat   horse   dog   _____

8. summer   spring   winter   _____

9. bat   ball   glove   _____

Answer these questions.

1. What three colors are on a traffic light?

_____

2. Which color tells us to STOP? _____

3. Which color tells us to GO? _____

4. Which color tells us to BE CAREFUL? _____

5. How many states are there in the U.S.A.? _____

6. What will a tadpole turn into? _____

7. What will a caterpillar turn into? _____

Match the person to the job.

firefighter	works in space
astronaut	works in a library
sailor	works in a school
librarian	works for the fire department
teacher	works in a hospital
doctor	works on a boat

Mixed Math

Add or subtract.

1.
3	7	8	6	6
+ 4	− 2	− 5	− 3	+ 3

2.
10	9	4	6	8
− 5	− 6	+ 7	+ 4	− 5

3.
11	7	12	2	6
− 6	+ 6	− 5	+ 7	+ 6

4. 9 − 4 = _____   10 − 7 = _____   4 + 5 = _____

5. 8 − 5 = _____   12 − 8 = _____   15 − 4 = _____

6. 10 + 6 = _____   9 + 3 = _____   13 − 7 = _____

Directions

1. Find Pennsylvania (PA) on the map. It is circled. Now find Oregon (OR). It is also circled.

   Pretend that you will drive from Pennsylvania to Oregon. Which direction will you drive: north, south, east, or west?

   _____

2. Now find Texas (TX). A square is drawn around it. Next, find North Dakota (ND). It also has a square.

   Pretend that you will fly from Texas to North Dakota. Which direction will you fly?

   _____

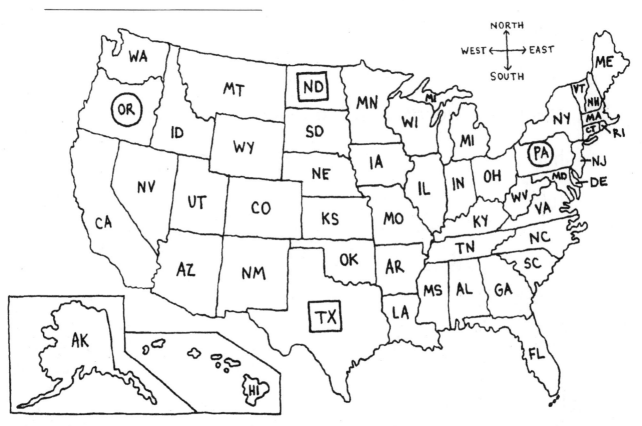

Long Sounds

1. Circle the words with the long sound of <u>e</u>.

   feet   pet   meat

   pea   web   tree

2. Circle the words with the long sound of <u>a</u>.

   late   map   dad

   rat   than   gate

3. Circle the words with the long sound of <u>i</u>.

   hid   kite   lid

   sit   five   bike

4. Circle the words with the long sound of <u>o</u>.

   goat   nose   top

   bone   pop   boat

5. Circle the words with the long sound of <u>u</u>.

   hug   cute   cut

   tub   suit   club

Short Sounds

1. Unscramble to find words with the short sound of a.

    a t c   <u>   cat   </u>   t f l a   <u>   </u>

    p p a l e   <u>   </u>   m p a   <u>   </u>

    r g a   <u>   </u>

2. Unscramble to find words with the short sound of e.

    h n e   <u>   hen   </u>   l b e l   <u>   </u>

    g g e   <u>   </u>   e d r   <u>   </u>

    b e w   <u>   </u>

3. Unscramble to find words with the short sound of i.

    g p i   <u>   pig   </u>   i f t g   <u>   </u>

    x i s   <u>   </u>   m t t i   <u>   </u>

    l k i m   <u>   </u>

4. Unscramble to find words with the short sound of <u>o</u>.

g o l   _____log_____   t p o   _____

o c k r   _____   b x o   _____

l l o d   _____

5. Unscramble to find words with the short sound of <u>u</u>.

b g u   _____bug_____   b u r   _____

s n u   _____   b u s r h   _____

p c u   _____

Write a word that rhymes with the word listed.
Then write a sentence using both words.

1. pig   _____big_____   A big pig fell into my

swimming pool this morning.

2. ball   _____   _____

_____

3. sun   _____   _____

_____

Seasons

In what season are these months?

1. January, February   _____

2. April, May   _____

3. July, August   _____

4. October, November   _____

Draw a picture of your favorite season.

Write about your picture.

_____

_____

_____

_____

Family

1. Write the names of your family below:

   _____   _____

   _____   _____

   _____   _____

2. All words have vowels (a, e, i, o, u, y).
   Circle the vowels in your family's names.

3. Write your family's names in alphabetical (ABC) order.

   _____   _____

   _____   _____

   _____   _____

4. Lauren can make the words *run* and *ran* from her name.
   Write the words you can make from your name here.

   _____   _____

   _____   _____

   _____   _____

Read About It Anthony discovers an "ant" in his name. Find out where Anthony discovers other "ants" by reading *There's an Ant in Anthony* by Bernard Most.

The Pilgrims

Long ago, the Pilgrims lived in England. The King of England did not allow them to go to their own church. So, they left England on a boat to come to America. The name of the boat was the *Mayflower*.

They landed at a place called Plymouth, Massachusetts. If you visit Plymouth today, you will see a rock where the Pilgrims landed.

Answer these questions about the Pilgrims.

1. The Pilgrims did not want to live in England because

_____

_____.

2. The Pilgrims came from (circle one)

America   England   Plymouth Rock

3. The Pilgrim's boat was called

_____.

4. The Pilgrims landed at

_____.

The first year in America was hard for the Pilgrims. They had very little food. The Indians taught the Pilgrims to plant corn, pumpkins, and beans. The Pilgrims thanked the Indians by having a feast. This was the first Thanksgiving.

5. The Indians taught the Pilgrims to

dance   sail   grow food

6. The Pilgrims thanked the Indians by

singing songs
having a feast
giving them corn

7. Plymouth is in Massachusetts. Find Massachusetts on the map on page 35 in this book.

Name two states that touch Massachusetts.

_____   _____

8. Write a sentence or two telling what your family does on Thanksgiving.

_____

_____

_____ .

Is It More or Less?

>   3 is greater than 2   3 > 2
=   3 is equal to 3   3 = 3
<   2 is less than 3   2 < 3

Fill in the blank with >, <, or = .

1. 10 > 9   6 ___ 5   7 ___ 10

2. 8 ___ 12   15 ___ 51   10 ___ 10

3. 25 ___ 52   19 ___ 20   54 ___ 54

4. 17 ___ 19   27 ___ 72   14 ___ 12

5. 25 ___ 25   67 ___ 64   35 ___ 36

6. 43 ___ 34   27 ___ 29   13 ___ 18

7. 2 + 4 ___ 1 + 3   3 − 2 ___ 6 + 3

8. 4 + 3 ___ 3 + 4   6 − 5 ___ 4 − 1

9. 6 + 2 ___ 3 + 5   7 + 3 ___ 3 + 7

Let's Alphabetize Our States!

1. Look at the map on the next page. Find 5 states that begin with <u>M</u>. Write them below.

   _____   _____

   _____   _____

   _____

2. Now put those same 5 states in ABC order.

   _____   _____

   _____   _____

   _____

3. Color your state red. Write the name of your state.

   _____

4. Write the names of the states that touch your state.

   _____

   _____

5. Color any states that you have visited green.

6. How many states are in the United States? _____

   How many have you visited? _____

   How many states do you have left to visit? _____

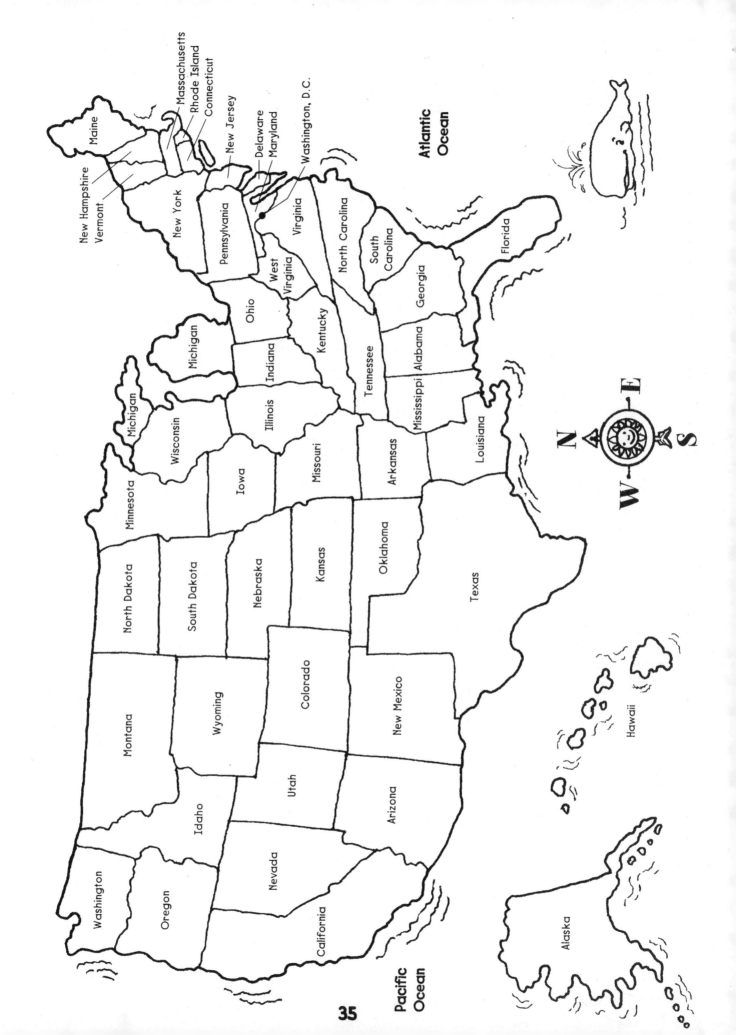

35

Planets

Look at the sun in the sky. Imagine that nine huge balls circle the sun. One is our planet, Earth. This page shows all nine planets and their names.

The sun is a star, because it shines by its own light. The planets do not shine by their own light. So, planets are not stars. Color the sun to show that it shines. Use the colors red, yellow, and orange.

Earth is mostly covered with water. Color Earth green to show land and BLUE to show water.

Venus is covered with clouds. Draw clouds around Venus, using black and blue.

Pluto

Neptune

Uranus

Saturn

Mercury

Mars

Sun

Venus

Earth

Jupiter

36

Saturn, Uranus, and Neptune have rings around them. Trace the rings around Saturn red. Trace the rings around Uranus blue. Trace the rings around Neptune yellow.

Pluto is the farthest away from the sun. It is cold on Pluto! Draw a snowman near Pluto to remind you that it is cold.

Earth is the only planet with people on it. But authors write pretend stories about people who come from Mars, called "Martians." Maybe E.T. was a Martian!

Draw a picture below to show what YOU think a Martian could look like!

MY FAVORITE MARTIAN

Before and After

Write the number or letter that comes before and after.

1. _7_, 8, _9_   8. ___, F, ___

2. ___, 14, ___   9. ___, M, ___

3. ___, 5, ___   10. ___, T, ___

4. ___, 9, ___   11. ___, J, ___

5. ___, 1, ___   12. ___, P, ___

6. ___, 6, ___   13. ___, L, ___

7. ___, 19, ___   14. ___, C, ___

Write the words that come before and after.

1. _____, Tuesday, _____

2. _____, Friday, _____

3. _____, August, _____

4. _____, March, _____

5. _____, summer, _____

6. _____, lunch, _____

JOKE CORNER

Why does a giraffe have a long neck?
See page 41 for answer.

Math Match

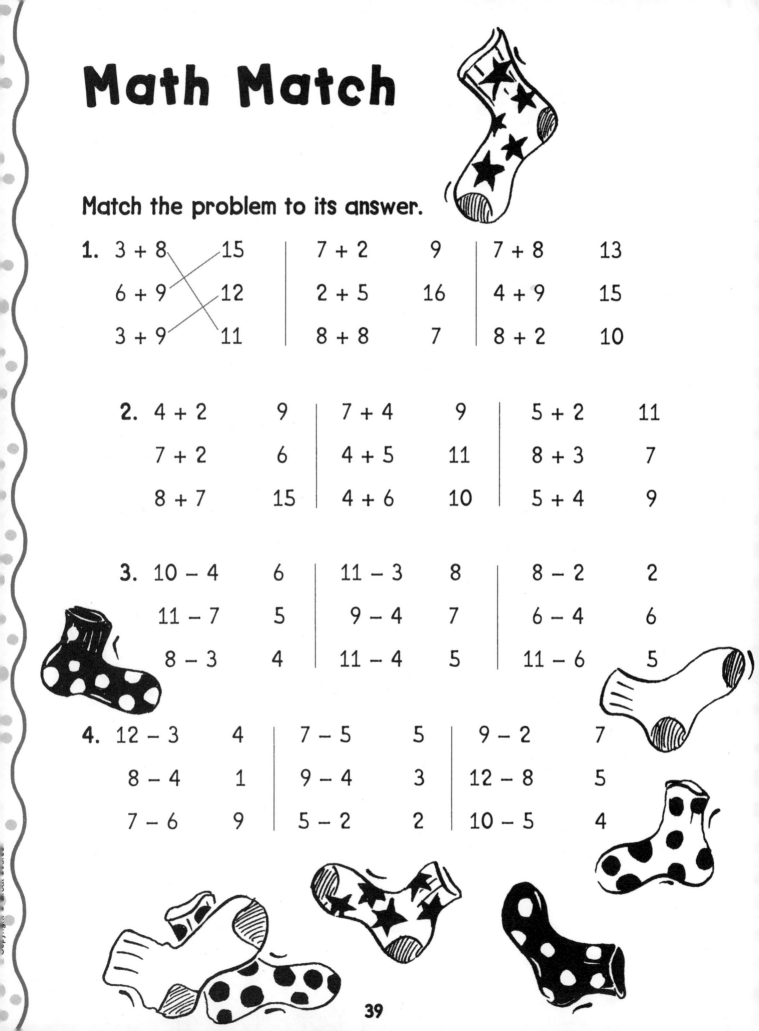

Match the problem to its answer.

1. 3 + 8   15 | 7 + 2   9 | 7 + 8   13
    6 + 9   12 | 2 + 5   16 | 4 + 9   15
    3 + 9   11 | 8 + 8   7 | 8 + 2   10

2. 4 + 2   9 | 7 + 4   9 | 5 + 2   11
    7 + 2   6 | 4 + 5   11 | 8 + 3   7
    8 + 7   15 | 4 + 6   10 | 5 + 4   9

3. 10 – 4   6 | 11 – 3   8 | 8 – 2   2
    11 – 7   5 | 9 – 4   7 | 6 – 4   6
    8 – 3   4 | 11 – 4   5 | 11 – 6   5

4. 12 – 3   4 | 7 – 5   5 | 9 – 2   7
    8 – 4   1 | 9 – 4   3 | 12 – 8   5
    7 – 6   9 | 5 – 2   2 | 10 – 5   4

39

Name Game

Let's have some fun with your name.

Here is a name poem written for **MARK.** Each letter is used to write a phrase to describe **MARK.** The first word in each phrase must start with the letter in **MARK's** name.

M any friends
A lways running
R eads a lot
K eeps rocks

Now it's your turn to try your own name poem.

Write your name in the column. Then write a word or phrase next to each letter that describes you. The first word in each phrase must start with a letter in your name.

Counting

1. Count by twos to fifty.

2, ___, 6, 8, ___, ___,

___, 16, ___, ___, ___,

___, 26, ___, ___, ___,

34, ___, ___, ___, ___,

44, ___, ___, 50

2. Add up the twos.

2 + 2 = ___

2 + 2 + 2 = ___

2 + 2 + 2 + 2 = ___

2 + 2 + 2 + 2 + 2 = ___

3. Count by fives to 100.

5, ___, 15, ___, 25, ___,

___, ___, ___, ___, ___,

___, ___, ___, ___, ___,

85, ___, ___, 100.

4. Add up the fives.

5 + 5 = ___

5 + 5 + 5 = ___

5 + 5 + 5 + 5 = ___

5 + 5 + 5 + 5 + 5 = ___

Joke answer from page 38:
Because he can't stand the smell of his feet.

41

5. Count by tens to 100.

10, ____, 30, ____, ____, ____, ____, 80, ____, 100.

6. Now count backwards by tens.

100, ____, ____, 70, ____, ____, 40, ____, ____, 10.

7. Add up the tens

$10 + 10 =$ ____

$10 + 10 + 10 =$ ____

$10 + 10 + 10 + 10 =$ ____

$10 + 10 + 10 + 10 + 10 =$ ____

8. Draw a line from the number to its name.

10	sixty
20	forty
30	seventy
40	ten
50	twenty
60	eighty
70	thirty
80	one hundred
90	fifty
100	ninety

Short a, e, i, o, u

Fill in the short vowels to name the pictures.

  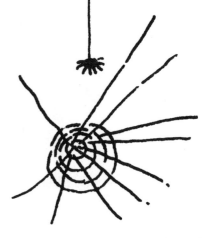

1. s __ x   s __ n   w __ b

2. p __ g   f __ n   h __ t

 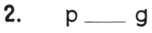 

3. c __ p   b __ g   g __ lf

Long a, e, i, o, u, y

Fill in the long vowel to name each picture.

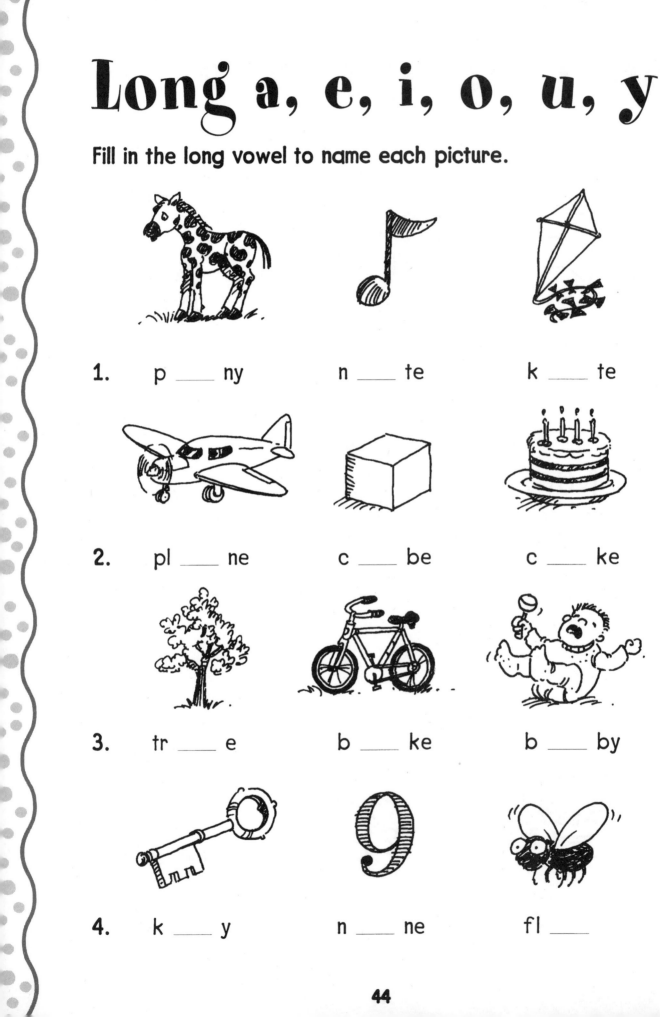

1.   p ___ ny   n ___ te   k ___ te

2.   pl ___ ne   c ___ be   c ___ ke

3.   tr ___ e   b ___ ke   b ___ by

4.   k ___ y   n ___ ne   fl ___

This and That

1. What comes next? first, second, third, _____

2. Which number is greater, 66 or 68? _____

3. Which number is less, 33 or 35? _____

4. What letter comes after M? _____

5. What number comes before 1? _____

6. What letter comes before Z? _____

7. How many pennies are in a dime? _____

8. How many pennies are in a quarter? _____

9. How many pennies are a dollar? _____

10. How many nickels are in a dime? _____

11. How many nickels are in a quarter? _____

12. How many nickels are in a dollar? _____

13. How many dimes are in a dollar? _____

14. What number comes before 100? _____

15. What number comes after 100? _____

16. What number comes after 99? _____

17. What number comes next? 1 , 3 , 5 , 7 , _____

18. What number comes next? 2 , 4 , 6 , 8 , _____

19. How many months are in a year? _____

20. How many days are in a week? _____

21. How many sides does a square have? _____

22. How many sides does a triangle have? _____

23. How many sides does a rectangle have? _____

24. How many letters are in the alphabet? _____

25. How much is 1 ten and 3 ones? _____

You Can Add!

Add the ones.
Then add the tens.

tens	ones		tens	ones
6	3		4	4
+	3		+2	3
6	6		6	7

1.

```
  22        47        54        66        33
 + 2       + 1       + 3       + 3       + 5
```

2.

```
  44        25        81        63        54
 +13       +11       +12       +14       +32
```

3.

```
  22        47        13        22        43
 +21       +42       +14       +36       +56
```

4. The Mets have 6 boys and 11 girls on their
team. How many players are on the team? _____

5. The Red Sox had 10 boys and 2 girls on
their team. 2 more girls joined the team. How
many players are on the team now? _____

47

All Grown Up

Write the other way of saying the underlined word or words.

Once upon a time there was a little child who was four years old. Mom would say, "Put on your shoes please." The child would say, "No, I <u>can't</u> (_____)". Mom would say, "Pick up your room please." The child would say, "I <u>don't</u> (_____) want to!" Mom would cry, "<u>I'd</u> (_____) like you to listen to me!" The child would say, "Sorry!"

Finally, the child grew up and <u>didn't</u> (_____) need as much help from Mom. Mom now says to the child, "<u>I'll</u> (_____) help you put on your shoes." The child says, "No, <u>I'll</u> (_____) do it myself!"

Read About It Read *You'll Soon Grow into Them, Titch* by Pat Hutchins, in which Titch finally becomes a big brother when a new baby is born.

You Can Subtract!

Subtract the ones. Then subtract the tens.

tens	ones
8	8
−	3
8	5

tens	ones
5	7
− 2	3
3	4

1.
```
  77        66        56        49        33
 - 3       - 2       - 6       - 5       - 1
```

2.
```
  67        49        35        18        54
 -22       -18       -12       -10       -21
```

3.
```
  47        36        28        55        82
 -25       -13       -14       -23       -12
```

4. The Phillies have 12 players on their team. On Saturday, 3 players are sick. How many players can play in Saturday's game? _____

5. The White Sox had 13 players on their team. Then 2 players moved away. How many players are left on the team? _____

49

Spell Check

Write the beginning and ending sounds to spell the words.

1. It comes after nine.   <u>t e n</u>

2. I sleep in it.   ___ e ___

3. We ride it to school.   ___ u ___

4. A spider lives in it.   ___ e ___

5. It keeps my head warm.   ___ a ___

6. It makes our days warm.   ___ u ___

7. Stop lights are this color.   ___ e ___

8. It burns in a fireplace.   ___ o ___

9. An ant or fly, for example.   ___ u ___

10. Fish use it to swim.   ___ i ___

The Father of Our Country

Before 1776, America belonged to the country of England. It was called a "colony" of England.

In 1776, America decided it did not want to belong to England. That started a war. The war was called the Revolutionary War. The leader of the American army was George Washington.

America won the war. It was no longer a colony of England. America thanked George Washington by making him the first president of the United States of America. George Washington's nickname is the "Father of Our Country."

1. What country did America belong to before 1776?

   _____

2. Why did Americans start the Revolutionary War?

   _____

   _____

3. Who led the American army?

_____

4. How did America thank George Washington?

_____

5. What is our nickname for George Washington?

_____

Mount Vernon

Bonus: The capital of the United States of America is named after George Washington. What is the capital of the United States of America?

_____

Telling Time

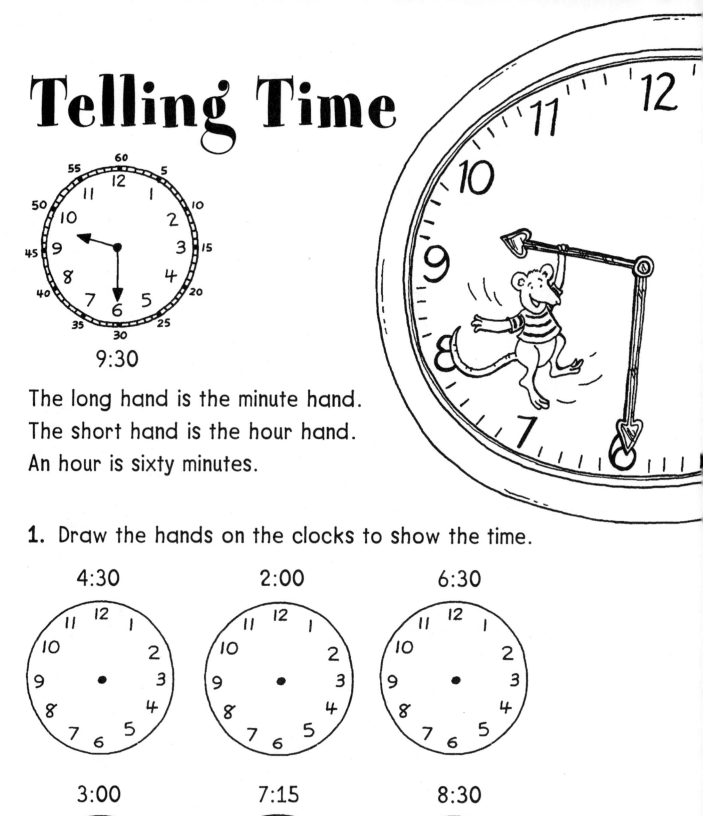

9:30

The long hand is the minute hand.
The short hand is the hour hand.
An hour is sixty minutes.

1. Draw the hands on the clocks to show the time.

4:30

2:00

6:30

3:00

7:15

8:30

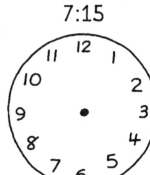

2. Write the correct time below each clock.

_____   _____   _____

_____   _____   _____

3. What is the correct time? Circle it.

Now

1 hour later

1 hour earlier

2 hours later

Prince Planet

Prince Planet does not know what the seasons are like in your state. He is going to visit you during your favorite season. Write a letter to Prince Planet to tell him about your season. What is the weather like? Do you go to school in that season? What will you and Prince Planet do when you play in that season?

Dear Prince Planet,

My favorite season is _____

_____

_____

_____

_____

_____

_____

Love,

_____
Write your name here.

Place Value

34 means 3 tens and 4 ones.

67 means 6 tens and 7 ones.

tens	ones
6	7

Tell how many tens and how many ones.

1. 29 = _____ tens and _____ ones.

2. 45 = _____ tens and _____ ones.

3. 53 = _____ tens and _____ ones.

4. 69 = _____ tens and _____ ones.

5. 77 = _____ tens and _____ ones.

6. 47 = _____ tens and _____ ones.

7. 76 = _____ tens and _____ ones.

8. 84 = _____ tens and _____ ones.

Fractions for Fun

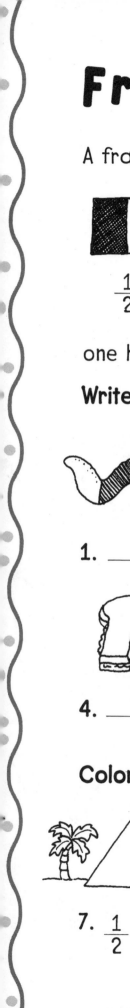

A fraction is part of something.

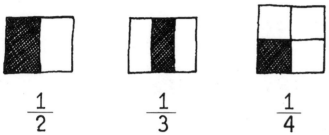

$\frac{1}{2}$ $\frac{1}{3}$ $\frac{1}{4}$

one half   one third   one fourth

Write the fraction for the shaded part.

1. _____   2. _____   3. _____

4. _____   5. _____   6. _____

Color the shapes to show the fractions.

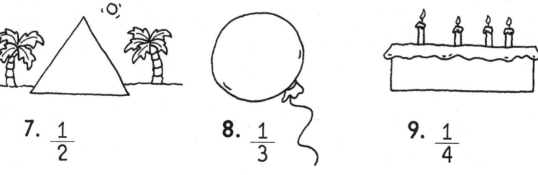

7. $\frac{1}{2}$ 8. $\frac{1}{3}$ 9. $\frac{1}{4}$

Coin Cents

A penny is worth one cent.   1¢
A nickel is worth five cents.   5¢
A dime is worth ten cents.   10¢
A quarter is worth twenty-five cents.   25¢

**Go get 10 pennies, 5 nickels, 2 dimes,
4 quarters. Using the coins you have, make**

1. 7¢   How many nickels? _____

            How many pennies? _____

2. 11¢   How many dimes? _____

            How many pennies? _____

3. 31¢   How many quarters? _____

            How many nickels? _____

            How many pennies? _____

4. 22¢   How many dimes? _____

            How many pennies? _____

**Let's say that you need a pencil for
second grade. It costs 20¢.**

1. If you used pennies, how many would you need? _____

2. If you used nickels, how many would you need? _____

3. If you used dimes, how many would you need? _____

4. If you used a quarter, how many coins would you get

   if your change was in pennies? _____

   if your change was in nickels? _____

Tell how many coins.

1. How many pennies in a dollar? _____

2. How many nickels in a dollar? _____

3. How many dimes in a dollar? _____

4. How many quarters in a dollar? _____

 **Read
About It** Find out all the things Alexander can
do with a dollar in *Alexander, Who Used
to be Rich Last Sunday* by Judith Viorst.

Word Games

Write a word that rhymes with each word below.

1. cat _____   4. ball _____

2. boy _____   5. house _____

3. book _____   6. bike _____

Draw a line from the word on the left to its opposite.

1. old   on

2. in   after

3. before   young

4. stop   go

5. she   he

6. off   out

Look at the pictures below.
Name each picture BIG, BIGGER, or BIGGEST.

_____   _____   _____

Take one word from the left and one word from the right to form a compound word.

class	board	1.	classroom
cow	room	2.	_____
rain	ship	3.	_____
bird	paste	4.	_____
skate	boy	5.	_____
pop	corn	6.	_____
space	cage	7.	_____
tooth	bow	8.	_____

Draw lines to connect words that mean ALMOST the same thing.

1. skinny   jacket

2. coat   cart

3. shirt   basement

4. wagon   blouse

5. cellar   thin

It's About Time

Answer these questions about time.

1. Sam ate dinner from 4 o'clock to 5 o'clock.

How long did Sam

eat dinner? _____ hour

from   to

2. Jane rode her bike from 2 o'clock to 5 o'clock.

How long did Jane

ride her bike? _____ hours

from   to

3. Tim swam from 1:30 o'clock to 3:30 o'clock.

How long did Tim

swim? _____ hours

from   to

Draw a line from each clock to the correct time.

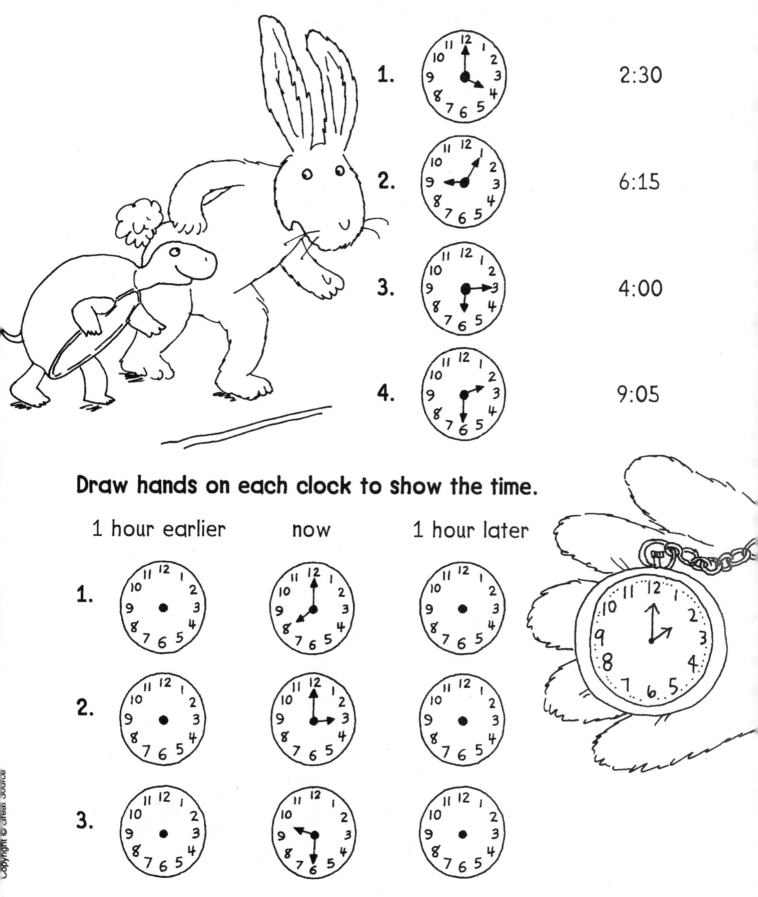

1.

2.

3.

4.

2:30

6:15

4:00

9:05

Draw hands on each clock to show the time.

1 hour earlier   now   1 hour later

1.

2.

3.

Plus or Minus

Write a plus sign or a minus sign in the circle.

1. 6 ⊕ 4 = 10
2. 5 ◯ 5 = 0
3. 10 = 7 ◯ 3
4. 6 ◯ 5 = 11
5. 14 = 7 ◯ 7
6. 9 = 5 ◯ 4
7. 8 ◯ 4 = 4
8. 12 = 9 ◯ 3
9. 10 ◯ 5 = 5

10. 5 ◯ 3 = 2
11. 6 ◯ 6 = 12
12. 8 = 7 ◯ 1
13. 7 ◯ 5 = 12
14. 8 ◯ 5 = 3
15. 11 ◯ 4 = 7
16. 10 = 6 ◯ 4
17. 2 ◯ 1 = 3
18. 5 ◯ 4 = 9

64

Adding Three Numbers

Add.

1.
4	5	3	6
3	5	7	3
+ 2	+ 5	+ 6	+ 4

2.
5	6	2	9
3	5	7	2
+ 4	+ 2	+ 3	+ 3

3.
7	8	3	6
6	4	4	3
+ 2	+ 5	+ 6	+ 5

Bonus: Which is larger, 1/2 or 1/3 of a hamburger?

What's The Story?

Finish the next three stories.

Goldilocks and the Three Bears

Beginning: Once upon a time there was a little girl named Goldilocks. She found a little house in the woods. She went inside.

Middle: She saw three bowls of porridge. Goldilocks tested the big bowl of porridge. It was too hot. Goldilocks tested the middle-sized bowl of porridge. It was too cold. Goldilocks tested the little bowl of porridge. It was just right. She ate all of it. Then Goldilocks saw three beds. She tested the big bed. It was too hard. Goldilocks tested the middle-sized bed. It was too soft. Then Goldilocks tested the little bed. It was just right. Goldilocks fell asleep.

End: _____

_____

_____

_____

_____

_____

The Three Little Pigs

Beginning: One day three little pigs went out to make themselves new homes. The first little pig built a weak house out of straw. The second little pig built a shaky house out of twigs. The third little pig worked much longer and harder. His house was strong. It was made from bricks.

Middle: _____

_____

_____

_____

_____

_____

_____

End: The wolf tried to huff, puff, and blow the third little pig's brick house down. The house was too strong. He tried to come down the chimney, but the third little pig had built a hot fire in the fireplace. The wolf ran away.

Little Red Riding Hood

Beginning: _____

_____

_____

_____

_____

_____

_____

Middle: Little Red Riding Hood got to Grandmother's house in the woods. The wolf was in Grandmother's bed, pretending to be her grandmother. Little Red Riding Hood saw that "Grandmother's" eyes, ears, and teeth were big.

End: The wolf jumped out of bed and chased Little Red Riding Hood. A woodcutter heard a lot of noise. He ran into Grandmother's house. He saved Little Red Riding Hood and Grandmother. He chased the wolf away.

Equal Sums

Circle the numbers that equal the sum at the top of the column.

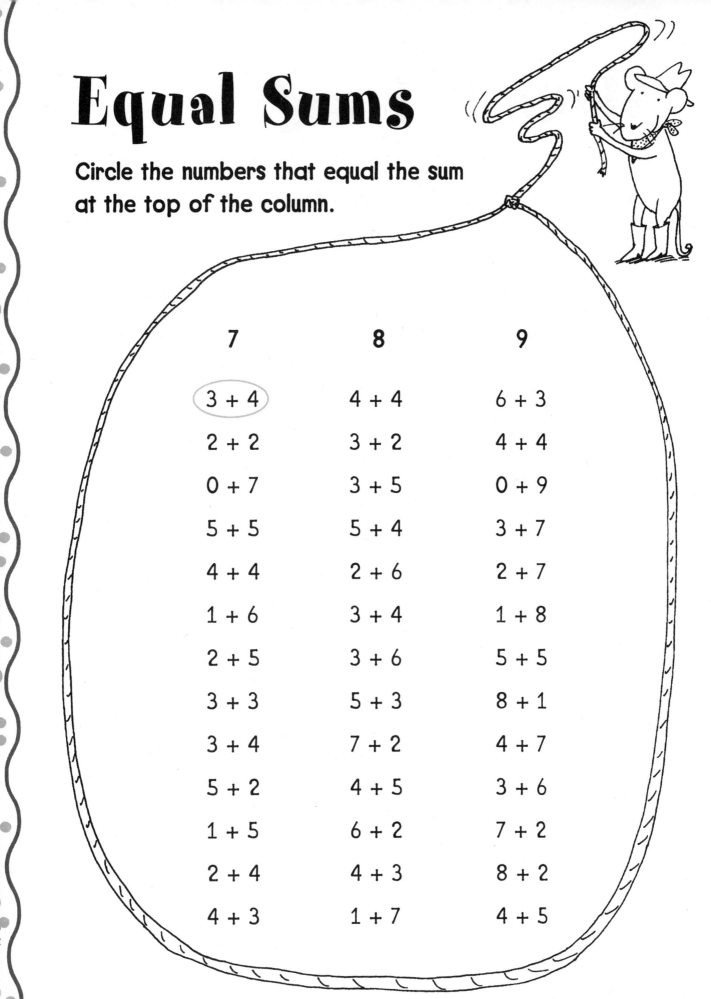

7	8	9
3 + 4	4 + 4	6 + 3
2 + 2	3 + 2	4 + 4
0 + 7	3 + 5	0 + 9
5 + 5	5 + 4	3 + 7
4 + 4	2 + 6	2 + 7
1 + 6	3 + 4	1 + 8
2 + 5	3 + 6	5 + 5
3 + 3	5 + 3	8 + 1
3 + 4	7 + 2	4 + 7
5 + 2	4 + 5	3 + 6
1 + 5	6 + 2	7 + 2
2 + 4	4 + 3	8 + 2
4 + 3	1 + 7	4 + 5

Make It Long!

Add an _e_ to the end of the underlined words to make the vowel sound long. Then write a sentence with your new word.

1. I <u>hid</u> from my brother this morning.

   _____

   _____

2. The mailcarrier's <u>cap</u> blew off his head and into the street.

   _____

   _____

3. Our soccer team had a <u>plan</u> to beat the Blue Jays.

   _____

   _____

4. My father gave me a <u>kit</u> to build a model airplane.

   _____

   _____

5. I am <u>not</u> going to swim team practice today.

   _____

   _____

Good Friends

Make new friends,
But keep the old.
One is silver and
The other gold.

1. This poem tells you to make new friends. What does the poet then tell you to do with your old ones?_____

_____

2. In the Olympics, what are the gold and silver medals for? _____

3. Which prize is more valuable, the gold or silver?

_____

4. Does the poet think that old friends or new friends are more like gold? _____

5. How do you think that new friends can turn from silver to gold? _____

6. Who is your oldest friend? _____

7. What is your favorite thing to do with this friend?

_____

8. Who is your newest friend? _____

9. Write three words to describe your new friend.

_____

What's That Sound?

<u>Th</u> is the sound in <u>thumb</u>. <u>Wh</u> is the sound in <u>whale</u>.
Finish spelling the words by writing <u>th</u> or <u>wh</u>.

1. ___ ___ ree

4. ___ ___ eel

2. ___ ___ ale

5. ___ ___ istle

3. sou ___ ___

6. ___ ___ row

72

S Blends

Fill in <u>sl</u>, <u>sk</u>, or <u>sn</u> to make new words.
Then choose one of the new words to draw
in the box below.

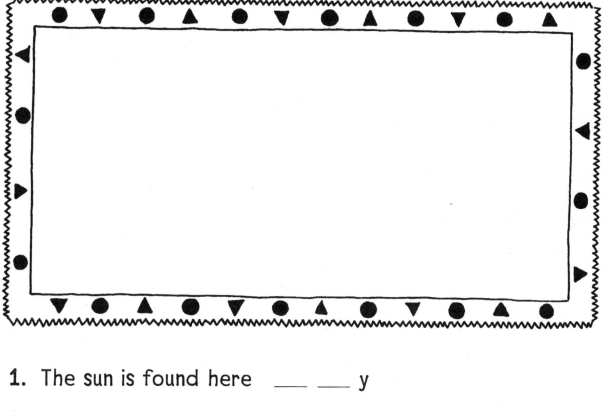

1. The sun is found here ___ ___ y

2. Like half a dress ___ ___ irt

3. Not fast, but ___ ___ ow

4. Falls from the winter sky ___ ___ ow

5. In-line skates do this ___ ___ ate

6. Do this at night ___ ___ eep

7. Covers our body ___ ___ in

8. Shoes for sports ___ ___ eakers

Finish spelling the words by using sm, sp, st, or sw.

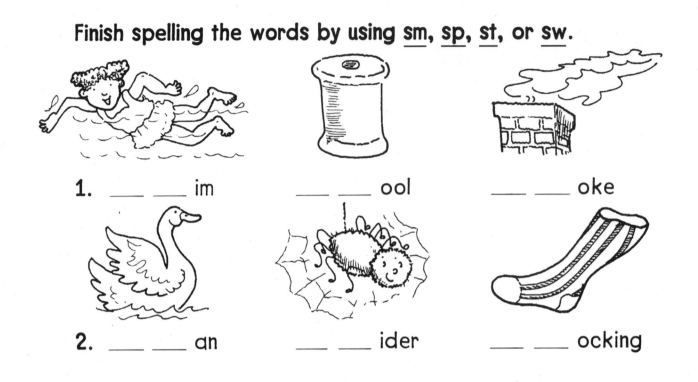

1. ___ ___ im   ___ ___ ool   ___ ___ oke

2. ___ ___ an   ___ ___ ider   ___ ___ ocking

Circle the words in the puzzle. The words go across and down.

ship   shoe   shop   shirt

dish   push   wash   brush

S H I P L S

H B R U S H

O W A S H I

E P K H O R

D I S H P T

74

Shhhhh.....

Circle the <u>sh</u> or <u>ch</u> in each word. Then, find the word that names each picture. Write the correct number in the circle.

1. shell

2. chest

3. church

4. cherries

5. shovel

6. shark

7. chipmunk

8. chicken

Riddles for Fun

Subtract to solve the riddles.

1. What do you call a dog at the beach?

Code:

1 = O	4 = C	7 = L
2 = G	5 = D	9 = K
3 = T	6 = H	10 = A

$$
\begin{array}{cccccc}
12 & 7 & 8 & 4 & 9 & 6 & 11 \\
-\ 2 & -\ 1 & -\ 7 & -\ 1 & -\ 4 & -\ 5 & -\ 9
\end{array}
$$

___ ___ ___ ___   ___ ___ ___

2. What has a face but cannot see?

$$
\begin{array}{cccccc}
12 & 6 & 12 & 10 & 9 & 11 \\
-\ 2 & -\ 2 & -\ 5 & -\ 9 & -\ 5 & -\ 2
\end{array}
$$

___   ___ ___ ___ ___ ___

Best of Summer

Draw a picture of the thing you enjoyed the
most this summer. Make it big and colorful!

Dear Teacher

Write a letter to your second grade teacher. Tell your teacher what you liked best about first grade. Then tell what was the hardest part of first grade. Finally, tell your second grade teacher what you are looking forward to in second grade.

Dear Second Grade Teacher,

_____

_____

_____

_____

_____

_____

_____

Signed,

_____

Your name

Book Section

The book section provides worksheets
for four books. Three are chosen.
The last one is a free choice.

Blaze Shows the Way by C. W. Anderson

Swamp Monsters by Mary Blount Christian

The Long Way to a New Land by Joan Sandin

Blaze Shows the Way

Read *Blaze Shows the Way* by
C. W. Anderson. Then, help our
cowboy blaze his way through the story trail.
Stories start by telling the reader the
SETTING of the story. The setting is
where and when the story takes place.

1. Circle the SETTING of *Blaze Shows the Way*.

   a. in faraway Greece, long, long ago
   b. out in the country, in the present time
   c. in a crowded city sometime in the future

2. Early on, the story introduces the major
   CHARACTERS. In *Blaze Shows the Way* the two
   major characters are boys. Who are they?

   _____ and _____

3. Next, the story describes a PROBLEM. Circle
   the problem in *Blaze Shows the Way*.

   a. Billy is tired of Tommy always following him.
   b. Because of the storm, the horse show is canceled.
   c. Tommy's horse is afraid to jump.

4. Finally, there is a SOLUTION to the problem. Circle the solution to the problem in *Blaze Shows the Way.*

    a. Dusty overcomes his fear of jumping during the storm.

    b. Tommy finally finds some friends his own age.

    c. Billy decides to ride in the horse show without Tommy.

Tommy really wanted to be like Billy. Billy was Tommy's **role model.** For some people, their role model is a famous basketball player or ballerina. But for many, a role model is a friend or family member.

Below, name someone who is a role model for you. Then tell at least one way that you would like to be like your role model.

ROLE MODEL

_____

_____

_____

_____

_____

Swamp Monsters

**Read *Swamp Monsters* by Mary Blount Christian.
After you read the book, answer the questions.**

1. What do Crag and Fenny, the monster
   children, eat for lunch?
   Crag and Fenny eat _____.

2. Instead of a dog, what do the monsters have?
   The monsters have _____.

3. Instead of reading books about monsters,
   what do monsters read books about?
   Monsters read books about _____.

4. Your mom might yell at you, "Stop acting
   like MONSTERS!" What does Mrs. Monster
   yell at her children?
   Mrs. Monster yells, _____.

5. When Crag and Fenny play dress-up, what
   do they dress like?
   The monsters dress like _____.

6. Who is the "tall one?"
   (Circle the correct answer.)

   a. She is the substitute teacher, Ms. Mumfrey.
   b. She is the biggest child in the class.
   c. She is the real teacher, Mrs. Smith.

7. What are the children doing in the swamp?
(Circle the correct answer.)

    a. They are on the playground.
    b. They are on a class trip.
    c. They live in the swamp.

8. Why doesn't Ms. Mumfrey know that Crag and Fenny are not in her class?
(Circle the correct answer.)

    a. She is not very smart.
    b. She is the substitute teacher.
    c. She thinks they are cute.

9. When Crag and Fenny go out to recess they see the children "hit that big white berry with a stick." What are the children doing?

_____

10. When Crag sees the children "swinging from a metal tree," what are the children doing?

_____

11. In the classroom, the children hear a scary story. What is it about?

_____

12. When Crag and Fenny get home, they hear a scary story. What is it about?

_____

This story uses compound words.
For example, a *storybook* is a book full of stories. A *lunchroom* is a place to eat lunch.

Use the clues to guess the following compound words.

1. Time to go to sleep _____ time

2. Opposite of inside _____ side

3. Falls from the sky _____ drops

    _____ flakes

4. Meeting place for club _____ house

5. Bird that is black _____ bird

6. Place to buy books _____ store

Story Starter: A story is started below.
Finish it with at least four complete sentences.

I always wanted to see what it would be like to live with swamp monsters. So, one night after my parents went to sleep, I snuck out of the house and headed to the graveyard. Soon, I heard a noise behind a gravestone, and _____

_____

_____

_____

The Long Way to a New Land

Get a copy of the book called
The Long Way to a New Land by Joan Sandin.

The book tells the story of a family who lived in Sweden over 100 years ago. The family lived on a farm. The farm was rocky and dry. The family could not grow food. They were hungry and without money. Finally the family decides to go to America to start a new life.

The book has 5 chapters. Stop after you read each chapter. Answer the questions about that chapter. You don't have to read this book in one day!

Chapter 1—The Letter from America

1. Why did the grass dry up, the cows stop giving milk, and the crops stop growing? _____

_____

2. What are the names of the boys in the book?

_____ and _____

3. What two things did Mama mix together to make their bread?

_____ and _____

4. Where is Uncle Axel?

_____

5. At the end of chapter 1, what does Pappa decide the family will do?

_____

_____

Chapter 2—Good-Bye to Sweden

Answer <u>yes</u> or <u>no</u>.

_____   **1.** Mamma and Pappa packed the family's things into a trunk with a lock.

_____   **2.** Farmor, Jonas' and Carl's grandmother, laughs when she kisses Jonas and Carl good-bye.

_____   **3.** At the end of chapter 2, Carl and his family get on a boat and say good-bye to Sweden.

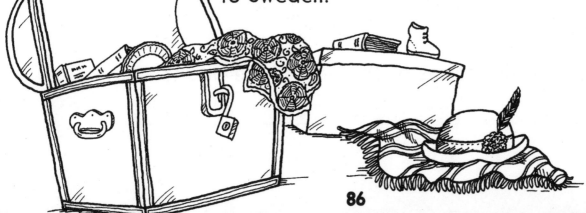

Chapter 3—Four Days to Liverpool

1. Where in the boat is the family staying? (on the deck? under the deck?)

   _____

2. After the boat takes the family to Hull, England, how does the family get to Liverpool, England?

   _____

3. Carl and his family speak Swedish. What other languages do the emigrants speak?

   _____

Chapter 4—Storm and Fever

Answer <u>yes</u> or <u>no</u>.

_____ 1. All the emigrants used clean cups or bowls to get fish stew from the kettle on the table.

_____ 2. The boat trip was rough. People got sick. Some died.

_____ 3. Carl and his family got a book to learn the English language.

Chapter 5—America at Last!

1. What did the men in uniforms do to the emigrants?

   _____

2. What did the doctor do to the emigrants?

   _____

3. What did Pappa find for his family that made him laugh?

   _____

Your parents, grandparents, great-grandparents, great-great-grandparents or great-great-great grandparents came by boat to America. Ask your parents what countries your family came from.

Countries my family came from: _____

_____

_____

_____

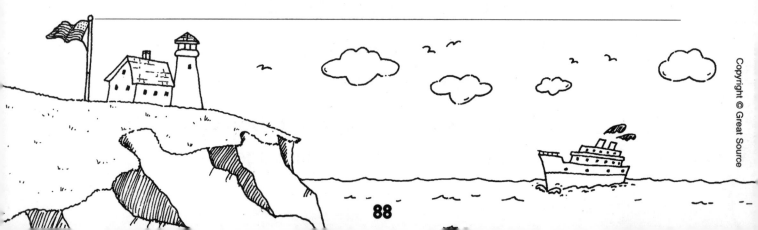

Any Old Book!

Find a book that you have not read, but would like to read. BEFORE you read the book, answer the following questions.

1. What is the title of your book? _____

2. What about the cover of the book makes you want to read it?

   _____

   _____

3. Who is the author of the book? _____

4. What do you think the book will be about?

   _____

   _____

Now, read the book and answer the following questions.

1. Who were the most important characters in your book?

   _____

2. Where did the story take place? _____

3. What surprised you about the story?

   _____

   _____

Answer Key

PAGE 6
8. red, white, blue

PAGES 9–10
1. Sunday, Monday, Tuesday, Wednesday, Thursday, Friday, Saturday
2. Friday, Monday, Saturday, Sunday, Thursday, Tuesday, Wednesday
3. Saturday, Sunday
4. 5
5. 7
6. d, a, y
7. 4, 1, 3, 2

PAGE 11
1. 0, 1, 2, 3, 4, 5, 6, 7, 8, 9. 10, 11, 12, 13, 14, 15, 16, 17, 18, 19, 20
2. 20, 19, 18, 17, 16, 15, 14, 13, 12, 11, 10, 9, 8, 7, 6, 5, 4, 3, 2, 1, 0
3. 1-one, 2-two, 3-three, 4-four, 5-five, 6-six, 7-seven, 8-eight, 9-nine, 10-ten, 11-eleven, 12-twelve, 13-thirteen, 14-fourteen, 15-fifteen, 16-sixteen, 17-seventeen, 18-eighteen, 19-nineteen, 20-twenty

PAGE 12
1. 8 cups
2. more sugar
3. 1 tablespoon

PAGE 13
1. 12
2. 2, 4, 7, 1, 8, 3, 11, 12, 5, 10, 9, 6
3-7. Answers vary.

PAGES 15–16
1. 8 11 9 10 8
2. 12 13 11 13 17
3. 10 10 16 16 10
4. 15 14 9
5. 7 14 9
6. 7 11 12
7. 3
8. 6
9. 14
10. 7 14

PAGES 19–20
1. 5 3 0 2 8
2. 4 3 3 4 5
3. 5 5 5 3 4
4. 7 2 8
5. 7 1 2
6. 1 6 4
7. 4 balloons
8. 4 stickers
9. 8 cards
10. 7 video games

PAGE 21
1. bone—stone
2. bat—that
3. dish—fish
4. car—star
5. peas—knees
6. dark—park

1. We were going to the beach.
2. My mother has red hair.
3. This fall, I will be in second grade.

PAGES 22–23
2. fruits
3. colors
4. months
5. clothing
6. days of the week
7. animals (mammals)
8. seasons
9. baseball equipment

1. red, yellow, green
2. red
3. green
4. yellow
5. 50 states
6. a frog or toad
7. a butterfly or moth

firefighter—works for the fire department
astronaut—works in space
sailor—works on a boat
librarian—works in a library
teacher—works in a school
doctor—works in a hospital

PAGE 24
1. 7 5 3 3 9
2. 5 3 11 10 3
3. 5 13 7 9 12
4. 5 3 9
5. 3 4 11
6. 16 12 6

PAGE 25
1. west
2. north

PAGE 26
1. feet, meat, pea, tree
2. late, gate
3. kite, five, bike
4. goat, nose, bone, boat
5. cute, suit

PAGES 27–28
1. apple, rag, flat, map
2. egg, web, bell, red
3. six, milk, gift, mitt
4. rock, doll, pot or top, box
5. sun, cup, rub, brush

PAGE 29
1. winter
2. spring
3. summer
4. fall or autumn

PAGES 31–32
1. They could not go to their own church.
2. England
3. the *Mayflower*
4. Plymouth, Massachusetts
5. grow food
6. having a feast
7. Possible choices: New Hampshire, Vermont, New York, Connecticut, Rhode Island

PAGE 33
1. 10 > 9   6 > 5   7 < 10
2. 8 < 12   15 < 51   10 = 10
3. 25 < 52   19 < 20   54 = 54
4. 17 < 19   27 < 72   14 > 12
5. 25 = 25   67 > 64   35 < 36
6. 43 > 34   27 < 29   13 < 18
7. >   <
8. =   <
9. =   =

PAGE 34
1. Possible answers: Montana, Minnesota, Missouri, Michigan, Mississippi, Massachusetts, Maryland, Maine
2. Possible answers: Maine, Maryland, Massachusetts, Michigan, Minnesota, Mississippi, Missouri, Montana

PAGE 38
2. 13, 14, 15
3. 4, 5, 6
4. 8, 9, 10
5. 0, 1, 2
6. 5, 6, 7
7. 18, 19, 20
8. E, F, G
9. L, M, N
10. S, T, U
11. I, J, K
12. O, P, Q
13. K, L, M
14. B, C, D

1. Monday, Tuesday, Wednesday
2. Thursday, Friday, Saturday
3. July, August, September
4. February, March, April
5. spring, summer, fall
6. breakfast, lunch, dinner or supper

PAGE 39
1. $3 + 8 = 11$
$6 + 9 = 15$
$3 + 9 = 12$

$7 + 2 = 9$
$2 + 5 = 7$
$8 + 8 = 16$

$7 + 8 = 15$
$4 + 9 = 13$
$8 + 2 = 10$

3. $10 - 4 = 6$
$11 - 7 = 4$
$8 - 3 = 5$

$11 - 3 = 8$
$9 - 4 = 5$
$11 - 4 = 7$

$8 - 2 = 6$
$6 - 4 = 2$
$11 - 6 = 5$

2. $4 + 2 = 6$
$7 + 2 = 9$
$8 + 7 = 15$

$7 + 4 = 11$
$4 + 5 = 9$
$4 + 6 = 10$

$5 + 2 = 7$
$8 + 3 = 11$
$5 + 4 = 9$

4. $12 - 3 = 9$
$8 - 4 = 4$
$7 - 6 = 1$

$7 - 5 = 2$
$9 - 4 = 5$
$5 - 2 = 3$

$9 - 2 = 7$
$12 - 8 = 4$
$10 - 5 = 5$

PAGES 41–42
1. 2, 4, 6, 8, 10, 12, 14, 16, 18, 20, 22, 24, 26, 28, 30, 32, 34, 36, 38, 40, 42, 44, 46, 48, 50
2. 4, 6, 8, 10
3. 5, 10, 15, 20, 25, 30, 35, 40, 45, 50, 55, 60, 65, 70, 75, 80, 85, 90, 95, 100
4. 10, 15, 20, 25
5. 10, 20, 30, 40, 50, 60, 70, 80, 90, 100
6. 100, 90, 80, 70, 60, 50, 40, 30, 20, 10
7. 20, 30, 40, 50
8. 10-ten, 20-twenty, 30-thirty, 40-forty, 50-fifty, 60-sixty, 70-seventy, 80-eighty, 90-ninety, 100-one hundred

PAGE 43
1. six, sun, web
2. pig, fan, hat
3. cup, bug, golf

PAGE 44
1. pony, note, kite
2. plane, cube, cake
3. tree, bike, baby
4. key, nine, fly

PAGES 45–46
1. fourth
2. 68
3. 33
4. N
5. O
6. Y
7. 10
8. 25
9. 100
10. 2
11. 5
12. 20
13. 10
14. 99
15. 101
16. 100
17. 9
18. 10
19. 12
20. 7
21. 4
22. 3
23. 4
24. 26
25. 13

PAGE 47
1. 24 48 57 69 38
2. 57 36 93 77 86
3. 43 89 27 58 99
4. 17
5. 14

PAGE 48
cannot
do not
I would
did not
I will
I will

PAGE 49
1. 74 64 50 44 32
2. 45 31 23 8 33
3. 22 23 14 32 70
4. 9
5. 11

PAGE 50
2. bed
3. bus
4. web
5. hat
6. sun
7. red
8. log
9. bug
10. fin

PAGES 51–52
1. England
2. America decided it did not want to belong to England.
3. George Washington
4. America thanked him by making him the first president
5. Father of Our Country
Bonus: Washington, D.C.

PAGE 54
2. 7:00 8:30 11:00
3:30 1:00 10:30
3. 8:00
2:00
7:00

PAGE 56
1. 2, 9
2. 4, 5
3. 5, 3
4. 6, 9
5. 7, 7
6. 4, 7
7. 7, 6
8. 8, 4

PAGE 57
1. $\frac{1}{3}$
2. $\frac{1}{4}$
3. $\frac{1}{2}$
4. $\frac{1}{2}$
5. $\frac{1}{4}$
6. $\frac{1}{3}$

91

PAGE 58

1. 1, 2
2. 1, 1
3. 1, 1, 1
4. 2, 2

PAGE 59

1. 20
2. 4
3. 2
4. 5, 1
5. 100
6. 20
7. 10
8. 4

PAGE 60

1.-6. Answers will vary.

1. old—young
2. in—out
3. before—after
4. stop—go
5. she—he
6. off—on

PAGE 61

1. classroom
2. cowboy
3. rainbow
4. birdcage
5. skateboard
6. popcorn
7. spaceship
8. toothpaste

1. skinny—thin
2. coat—jacket
3. shirt—blouse
4. wagon—cart
5. cellar—basement

PAGE 62

1. 1 hour
2. 3 hours
3. 2 hours

PAGE 63

1. 4:00
2. 9:05
3. 6:15
4. 2:30

PAGE 64

1. $6 + 4 = 10$
2. $5 - 5 = 0$
3. $10 = 7 + 3$
4. $6 + 5 = 11$
5. $14 = 7 + 7$
6. $9 = 5 + 4$
7. $8 - 4 = 4$
8. $12 = 9 + 3$
9. $10 - 5 = 5$
10. $5 - 3 = 2$
11. $6 + 6 = 12$
12. $8 = 7 + 1$
13. $7 + 5 = 12$
14. $8 - 5 = 3$
15. $11 - 4 = 7$
16. $10 = 6 + 4$
17. $2 + 1 = 3$
18. $5 + 4 = 9$

PAGE 65

1. 9 15 16 13
2. 12 13 12 14
3. 15 17 13 14

Bonus: $\frac{1}{2}$

PAGE 69

7: 0 + 7 1 + 6 2 + 5 3 + 4 5 + 2 4 + 3
8: 4 + 4 3 + 5 2 + 6 5 + 3 6 + 2 1 + 7
9: 6 + 3 0 + 9 2 + 7 1 + 8 8 + 1 3 + 6 7 + 2 4 + 5

PAGE 72

1. three
2. whale
3. south
4. wheel
5. whistle
6. throw

PAGE 73

1. sky
2. skirt
3. slow
4. snow
5. skate
6. sleep
7. skin
8. sneakers

1. swim spool smoke
2. swan spider stocking

```
S H I P L S
H B R U S H H
O W A S H I
E P K H O R
D I S H P T
```

PAGE 76

1. 10 6 1 3 5 1 2   A hot dog
2. 10 4 7 1 4 9   A clock

PAGE 80

1. b
2. Tommy and Billy
3. a
4. b

PAGE 82

1. snail stew
2. an alligator
3. children
4. "Stop acting like children!"
5. children
6. She is the substitute teacher, Ms. Mumfrey.
7. They are on a class trip.
8. She is the substitute teacher.
9. They are playing baseball.
10. They are playing on the jungle gym.
11. It is about monsters.
12. It is about children.

PAGE 84

1. bedtime
2. outside
3. raindrops, snowflakes
4. clubhouse
5. blackbird
6. bookstore

PAGES 85–88

Chapter 1
1. because there was no rain
2. Carl Erik and Jonas
3. bark and flour
4. He is in America
5. go to America

Chapter 2
1. yes
2. no
3. yes

Chapter 3
1. under the deck
2. They take a train.
3. English, German, Norwegian, Italian, French

Chapter 4
1. no
2. yes
3. yes

Chapter 5
1. The men examined their baggage.
2. He looked into their eyes and down their throats. He thumped their chests.
3. wheat bread with butter